Izzy's Secret Project

By Spencer White

Izzy went to visit Gran.

“Gran, I want to give Dad a scarf for his birthday, but I cannot find one I like,” said Izzy.

“I can teach you the method for knitting a basic scarf,” said Gran.

“Great!” Izzy cried.
“I’ll be a good student!”

Izzy picked some yellow yarn.

“The first lesson is to knit a small piece, as a trial,” said Gran.

She showed Izzy how to knit a row.

Izzy did not start well.

She got upset.

Then the yarn snapped in her hands.

"Don't panic!" said Gran. "You'll get the hang of it."

With Gran to assist, Izzy's secret project began to look great.

"I'll finish this scarf in no time!" said Izzy.

Izzy could see Dad outside through the window.

So she had time to stuff the scarf into her jacket pocket before he came inside.

Once, Dad walked into Izzy's bedroom while she was knitting.

Izzy had to hide the scarf under the doona!

The night before Dad's birthday, Izzy called Gran.

"I finished it!" she whispered.

"What a triumph!" said Gran. "You are my best student!"

The next morning, Izzy gave Dad his present.

“I love it!” Dad said. “You have a real talent for knitting!”

“I’ll make you matching mittens next,” Izzy said.

CHECKING FOR MEANING

1. What was Izzy's secret project? *(Literal)*
2. Who taught Izzy to knit a basic scarf? *(Literal)*
3. Why did Izzy want to keep the knitting project a secret from Dad? *(Inferential)*
4. How do you think Izzy felt about making Dad a present for his birthday instead of buying one? *(Evaluative)*

EXTENDING VOCABULARY

method	Where do you divide the syllables in the word *method*? What is a method? What kind of activity needs a method?
stuff	If you stuff something into your pocket, do you put it there carefully or messily?
whispered	What do you do with your voice when you whisper? What is the opposite of *whisper*?

MOVING BEYOND THE TEXT

1. What types of art or craft projects have you done? What kinds of crafts do you enjoy or want to try?
2. Izzy thought her scarf was ruined because she made a mistake. How can you get better at something and make fewer mistakes?
3. When have you felt a sense of triumph?
4. Tell me about a time you surprised someone. How did they feel about it? Have you ever been surprised?

TIME TO WRITE

Write the next part of the story. What might have happened next on Dad's birthday?